SHANE W. EVANS

WE MARCH

A NEAL PORTER BOOK
ROARING BROOK PRESS
NEW YORK

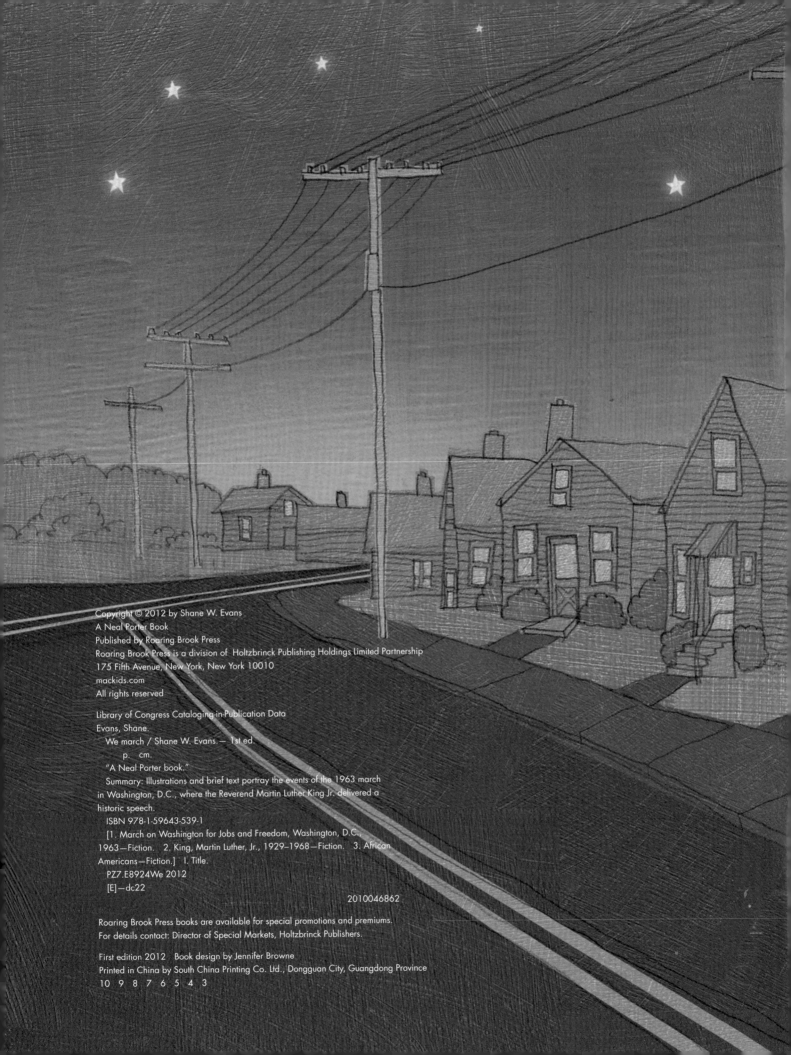

Copyright © 2012 by Shane W. Evans
A Neal Porter Book
Published by Roaring Brook Press
Roaring Brook Press is a division of Holtzbrinck Publishing Holdings Limited Partnership
175 Fifth Avenue, New York, New York 10010
mackids.com

Library of Congress Cataloging-in-Publication Data
Evans, Shane.
    We march / Shane W. Evans.— 1st ed.
        p.   cm.
    "A Neal Porter book."
    Summary: Illustrations and brief text portray the events of the 1963 march
in Washington, D.C., where the Reverend Martin Luther King Jr. delivered a
historic speech.
    ISBN 978-1-59643-539-1
    [1. March on Washington for Jobs and Freedom, Washington, D.C.,
1963—Fiction.   2. King, Martin Luther, Jr., 1929–1968—Fiction.   3. African
Americans—Fiction.]   I. Title.
    PZ7.E8924We 2012
    [E]—dc22
                                                        2010046862

Roaring Brook Press books are available for special promotions and premiums.
For details contact: Director of Special Markets, Holtzbrinck Publishers.

First edition 2012   Book design by Jennifer Browne
Printed in China by South China Printing Co. Ltd., Dongguan City, Guangdong Province
10 9 8 7 6 5 4 3

The morning is quiet.

The sun rises

and we prepare

to march.

We pray for strength.

We come from all over . . .

to march.

We follow our leaders.

We walk together.

We sing.

We are hot and tired,
but we are filled with hope.

We lean on each other

as we march to justice,

to freedom,

to our dreams.

On August 28, 1963, more than 250,000 people gathered in our nation's capital to participate in the March on Washington for Jobs and Freedom. The march began at the Washington Monument and ended with a rally at the Lincoln Memorial, where iconic musicians such as Mahalia Jackson, Bob Dylan, and Joan Baez performed, and Martin Luther King Jr. delivered his historic "I Have a Dream" speech.

Throughout history, there have been many organized marches when people walked together to advance a common goal. The Selma to Montgomery March, which consisted of three separate marches that took place in March of 1965, was held to focus attention on the Civil Rights Movement and the need for outlawing racial discrimination. The routes are now memorialized as the Selma To Montgomery Voting Rights Trail.

Following these marches, the country enacted two pieces of legislation that were crucial for moving the country toward racial equality. The first was the Civil Rights Act of 1964, which banned racial segregation in public schools, public places, and in select workplaces. The second was the National Voting Rights Act of 1965, which outlawed discriminatory voting practices that denied many African Americans the right to vote.

It takes people of all ages and cultural backgrounds to move a nation into a new era of freedom. In a sense, these marches pushed old ideas out of the way and moved new ideas forward. History shows that where there is change, there will often be resistance to change. However, these events demonstrate that through action and determination people have the power to overcome that resistance.

I have always been inspired by the idea of people coming together, joining hands in prayer, lifting their voices in song, and marching toward freedom.

Shane W. Evans